PRAYER FOR TIME

PRAYER FOR TIME

A MEMOIR

WILLIAM R. MONTGOMERY

Sandra,
May the road
rise to meet your
feet
Bull
9/14

This memoir is dedicated to the life of Arnold Van Zanten

Contents

PROLOGUE

Dear Lord,
Thank You for this day and for the gift of Your creation.

It is early May when my wife Anne and I turn north off M-72 and head for the family cottage on Lake Skegemog. At the top of the first hill we pull to the side of the road to enjoy our first Skegemog view of the season—the same shimmering expanse that greeted my family in June of 1949, when my parents first drove this same road. At the time, we all lived in Detroit so my brother Tom and I had little contact with lakes, although we once vacationed at Aunt Lil's home on Lake Erie. With me going on eight and Tom about four, we were beginning what would become 64 straight summers on a northern Michigan lake.

Today, the shore of our 2-mile wide by 3-mile long lake appears much the same as when Mother and Dad were first attracted to this territory, with the eastern end largely comprised of wetlands and therefore void of human structures. These days, the wetlands are our favorite place to kayak and look for Sand Hill Cranes while the western end has many cottages set in a woodsy environment.

The state owns half of the lake thus preserving the rural quality of the area.

Even in the warm spring sun the water presents a seasonal steel-gray view. This May morning I look forward to seeing a bright blueness return to the lake, and anticipate the arc of the sun as it moves higher in the sky.

May we preserve the precious land
as well as have our predecessors.

Most of the land on the left hand side of the road is cherry orchard, although there's also a cornfield, planted in response to the demand for ethanol. I notice the raised hunting blind to the left, and muse about who uses it, imagining deer and pheasants passing through the sleeping fields in the fall.

The right hand side of the road is marked by meadows and about a half dozen houses. The first we see is an old farmhouse that's occasionally occupied but seems empty at this time. The deteriorating white paint on its two story square structure reminds me of my Uncle Elmer and Aunt Hazel's Ohio farmhouse which I visited during the 1940s and early 1950s. I was saddened to hear that after they passed away, their house was set afire by the local fire department for a training exercise.

Most of the cottages along the lake are not visible until we clear the crest of the last hill, then come to the T in the road about 100 yards from the lakeshore. All of the cottages, set on 70 to 100 foot lots, have seasonal docks that extend out into the water, connecting boat hoists to the shore.

We turn right onto Hoiles Road, named after Sam Hoiles, who originally farmed many of the cherry orchards we have just driven past; we go three-eights of a mile and turn into the two-track driveway to our cottage. Leaving the car, we walk past our red garage, built at least 50 years ago by a neighbor whose 90th birthday we helped celebrate just three days ago. Soon after we arrive, we'll place furniture on the deck and porch, activate the irrigation system, raise shades and open all the doors for the season. First, I walk around the house to the lake.

The lake symbolizes the stabilizing nature of this place for our family, providing a view that's remained virtually the same over all the years we've come here. The land across the lake is still virgin and the shore of our property has not changed. It is as though I am standing in a time-warp and have the privilege to "re-boot" my feelings to an earlier, simpler time. I recall what one of the kids said recently, "You can sell the Dallas house if you want, but never, never sell the cottage as it is where the soul of the family resides." I turn around to admire the cottage from the front, dominated as it is by two-story windows and a screened-in porch. It is here that I will ponder the issue of what kind of person I am and what kind of person I will become, now that the reality of cancer is a constant presence in my thoughts. I want to have these issues clearly before me as I sit in the peace of the cottage, and plan for the time ahead.

Thank You for bringing Mother and Dad
to this part of the world.

Four generations of our family have used the cottage for over forty years. Mother and Dad bought it in the early 70s and since that time my parents, my brother and I, our wives, our children and their children have all vacationed here. This summer my brother and I plan to convert the ownership of the cottage into a legal form that will simplify the way stewardship will be passed from generation to generation. The next generation will consist of six owners instead of my brother and me.

When we replaced the cottage structure in 2003 by sticking within the footprint of the original, we achieved a year-round home without removing any of the nearly 100 year-old towering oak or maple trees. The remaining mature trees are a reminder of the time that the property has been in the family and the permanence of this place. While I am dismayed to see the ten insect-infested ash trees that the tree surgeon marked for removal, I feel good about the variety of young trees that we will replace them with. My preference is to continue planting pine trees as Tom, Dad and I began to do 35 years ago. I wish we had planted more, back then, given all they've added to this property, and in exchange for such little effort.

May we live in harmony with the other creatures
and plants that share this land.

Coming back each year, we are made constantly aware of the wildlife in our midst: deer, wild turkey, raccoons, squirrels, chipmunks, and even the occasional foraging bear give witness to the importance of nature, and add to the rustic aura of the cottage. This spring, the half-eaten branches of shrubs tell me the deer suffered a tough winter, but bald eagles have returned for the summer, and I see their outline extending at least two feet above their nest, which I estimate to be about eight feet across. I hope they will make their usual late afternoon fishing glide-by on our side of the lake.

I ask Your help in keeping my health problems at bay
that I might live in Your grace to be a part of the lives
of my grandchildren and possible great-grandchildren.

I am fighting advanced prostate cancer (APC), which occurs when the disease returns, despite the initial treatment. In my case, the prostate was surgically removed in 2008 and within a year, cancer was again detected in my bloodstream. This type of cancer, while often fatal, is treatable with drugs and radiation aimed at postponing the growth and spread of the disease. I know that we all must die at some point, but a true sense of urgency followed my diagnosis. I now recognize the potential for an early death and want to maximize my actions between now and the end of my life so that I can leave my survivors with additional memories. I also need a plan to deal with this reality.

I need to make clear how I want my life to bear witness among my surviving family and friends. In addition to knowing that I enjoy golf, traveling, reading and eating in good restaurants, I want my survivors to know that I loved them all, aspired to help those less fortunate than myself, and tried to lead a Christian life. Further, I want my survivors to know that I believe that my life has benefited from several instances of divine intervention, some sudden and even dramatic, as well as the immeasurably positive impact of marrying Anne. I want to communicate my belief in the power of education, and describe my effort to follow my mother's admonition to "advance the line." All of these values have played out in my life and I hope that reflecting upon a few defining forces and events will put me on the path to a productive use of the remainder of my time.

May the Lord grant me insight to complete
my intended mission.

I unpack the car and move bags of groceries, clothing, computer, printer, paper, pens and several favorite books into the cottage. We will stay three weeks and I intend to use this time to read, reflect and plan. Anne will work in the cottage gardens and also spend time reading. My workspace is an open area on the second floor where I position my table to allow a direct view of the lake through large windows. I am ready to begin. I am home.

AMEN

1.

THE MAJOR SHAPERS

Dear Lord,
Thank You for the loving family members, friends and
colleagues who have shaped the way that I view this world.

Like all personalities, I am a reflection of the influences around me. My mother, father, both grandmothers, a lone grandfather and brother were significant forces that shaped me during my formative years, while early in my adult life I met and married Anne, my wife, partner, best friend, confidant and advisor for more than four decades. Through a process that calls to mind a craftsman with sandpapers of different roughness working the wood into the shape he seeks, each of my "major shapers" has marked me in meaningful ways.

My parents focused the basic beliefs I brought to my marriage in which Anne and I became the parents, teachers, and framers of three children, Alyson, John and Chris, as well as to our five grandchildren, Alex, Amelia, Lucy Kate, Kyle and Jay.

My maternal grandparents, Myron and Edna, had a major influence because we all lived in the same Detroit neighborhood until our move to the suburbs when I was in the eighth grade. Myron emigrated from Ireland, arriving in Detroit via Canada. There was a lot of anti-Irish Catholic prejudice in Detroit in the years after World War I so in order to get work in the post office he said he was a Methodist from Canada. It was in the neighborhood Methodist Church that my grandparents, and subsequently my parents, met and married.

I will always remember Myron as frugal. When I was probably five or six, he told me he needed some help so I followed him down the alley behind his house to a place where someone had thrown away a large, barely alive, five-foot shrub. He picked it up by the roots and I carried a few branches up to the front of his house where we took turns digging a hole, and finally planting it. My grandmother was furious because of the scrounging nature of the tasks he had me do, and because she thought that all the neighbors would know where the half dead bush came from. Grandpa, on the other hand, nursed that shrub back to life and it lived longer than he did. As I write this, I realize that Anne and I have combined to continue Myron's frugality, a fact that has helped to make our retirement so financially comfortable.

My father's parents were English, however, I have no memory of my grandfather, Ora, who died when I was very young. A picture of him holding me as a baby is the only thread to him. Dad's mother, Estelle, was a very formal, serious, and strict person who lived a couple of miles from our neighborhood. As you might imagine, with the parts of the family in such close proximity, seeing the grandparents at church, followed by family dinners, was the usual order of our Sunday. I remember those meals in Estelle's second floor apartment as adult oriented affairs in contrast to the relaxed atmosphere of Myron and Edna's Sunday dinners.

Reflecting his parent's sensibilities, my father was a very private and somewhat formal man himself, who always felt that personal issues, particularly medical problems, should not be discussed outside the family; it was not our practice to even talk about a family pregnancy with outsiders. My brother and I were given a real example of love when Dad took care of Mother as she suffered with Alzheimer's disease, and was unresponsive for years. We were surprised to see a video of our usually private father being interviewed on local television about the experience of caring for our mother. We felt a great sense of pride and admiration as we watched Dad discuss Mother's condition and his response to the disease in the such a public context. We saw his devotion to her override his personal privacy policy. I hope that many people were inspired by his interview.

Mother believed that everyone in the family should "advance the line." She meant that we should provide our children with opportunities that were greater than those we had received, included educational experiences and the ability to make greater contributions to society. During the early years of The Depression, Mother's family could only afford to fund one education so the decision was made to send her brother, Jack, to college, then medical school. Everyone else in the family worked to support that decision. As a result, my uncle Jack became an influential and successful doctor who started a medical clinic now consisting of over 25 doctors. Naturally, Tom and I were expected to do well in the best schools. In fact, education was so important that it was for this reason that our family moved out of the long-time family neighborhood in Detroit to give us a better opportunity in a suburban school system.

I have always understood my parent's wishes and I want the same for our children. "Advancing the line" and our shared belief in the great value of education are concepts which actually overlap each other. We hope our children will be well educated and make a more profound contribution to the world than that we were able to make.

Of course, all of these big ideas were made possible by the fact that I found the right partner in Anne, whom I met for the first time playing volleyball at the usual Wednesday evening game in Lincoln Park on Chicago's near north side. I had moved to that neighborhood in the spring of 1966, after a year in Evanston, during which time I had dated several women, though I had not come across the ideal mate. During that time, friends often mentioned a woman that they wanted me to meet. Her name was Anne.

Anne and I left the volleyball game together that evening, taking the equipment to the local bar to be stored. Imagine my surprise when she turned out to be THE Anne. Our first date was the next week when the top brass of my employer needed a couple to fill in a table at a political fundraiser. On short notice, Anne and I appeared at the formal event, she dressed in a soft pink suit with a white blouse and I in the expected blue suit, a white button down shirt and the appropriately shaded red tie. I could not believe how poised and comfortable she was at this important social affair and later we both enjoyed our first goodnight kiss. About six weeks later, returning from a visit to meet my parents, I mentioned marriage for the first time. There was never any doubt. We had found the right partner in each other.

Who knows what causes a love to develop and flourish. One important element must be the continual discovery of previously unknown attributes of the object of one's love. Many things about Anne struck me as desirable: she made poached eggs with just the right firmness, read widely, had fun friends, was beautiful, possessed a great deal of common sense, and was good at whatever she tried including golf, child raising, plumbing, managing cross country moves and decorating. Marrying Anne on July 29th, 1967 was the smartest thing I have ever done. Period.

One of the most important but unspoken, aspects of our marriage was the covenant of roles. We both had been raised to believe that it was the man's job to earn the living and the woman's job to raise the children and manage the family. While we have modified the role on many occasions over the years, that view largely reflects the way that we lived, and that basic understanding has helped us avoid a lot of the difficulties facing other marriages. Retirement and uncertainties concerning my health have blurred our roles and we now work to share almost all responsibilities in a constantly changing give and take.

I like to think family structure can be represented with a solar system model. The role of the sun in this model is the religious concept of the source of life. Any single life, such as mine, is represented by the planet earth, which has the environment in which billions of us can flourish. The four large outer planets represent the major shapers of my life and way of living, that is: Mother, Dad, Tom and Anne. The smaller planets and their moons, represent, in various combinations, those we shape such as our children and grandchildren. Comets are things whose entry into our lives can be either good or bad but are beyond our control. They enter our system and then move on. There are several useful aspects of this model. It underlines my view that the focus of our lives should be our children and their children, represented by the smaller inner planets that orbit between the earth and sun. The large outer planets show the importance that parents and spouses have had upon our lives. The sun and its overwhelming gravitational pull represent our religious base of life and the force that binds us all together.

As I sit and reflect upon this model, I look through the windows and see Anne at work in the garden. She has already pruned back the hydrangea plants that threatened to overrun the eastern end of the porch; she has trimmed the Iris, Cat's Paw and Spirea. By the location of the tools, I see that it is time for me to help with the annual installation of the irrigation pump. I lay my pencil down and head out to the lawn.

2.

A REFOCUSING DIAGNOSIS

Dear Lord,
Please comfort those who receive a cancer diagnosis.

There is a commonly accepted definition of time: The measured or measurable period during which an action, process or condition exists or continues. I have begun to think a lot more about the value of time and how I will use my remaining days, months and years. In fact, I wonder if I have begun to obsess on the subject.

My study of prostate cancer led me to believe my situation would be readily corrected by a minor surgery that might produce mild side effects. Several doctors I consulted reinforced my upbeat view of the surgical alternative I chose. I went forward with surgery in Traverse City, optimistic that the threat would disappear from my life following a successful removal of the prostate. In the months that followed, I was delighted by the way my life returned to normal. There were relatively minor side effects and I was pleased to have beaten cancer. I golfed two or three times a week, walked several miles at a time for exercise, and resumed all the pre-cancer activities I enjoyed. This euphoria was short lived, however. Nine months after surgery we were set to leave Dallas for Michigan when I got the call from the nurse of my long time internist who had just given me a physical exam the previous day.

Teresa said, "It's not often that we see a PSA number as low as 0.2. You should be proud."

"Teresa," I responded, more than a little upset. "It should be zero. Remember, I had my prostate removed."

My internist picked up the call quickly saying, "Get right down here and we will draw another sample. If you hurry, we will get the results back yet this afternoon."

I immediately drove to his office, had another test drawn, and we did get the confirming answer that afternoon. Jeff reported that the test results were the same. "While the PSA test yields only a symptom of cancer, it is the best that we have. As soon as you get to Traverse City, go talk with your surgeon."

I remember the long drive to Traverse City as the first time we faced the worry of cancer truly impinging upon our lives. I had done enough reading about prostate cancer in general to be able to tell Anne some of the basics that would become so familiar to both of us.

"Houston, we have a problem," I said, trying to make somewhat light of the situation.

"Don't be cute", she quickly responded, "What do we know with certainty?"

"Well, Jeff said that the PSA measurement is small enough that APC is not for sure but only a possibility. He said we should relax and wait for the another blood test in a few weeks," I replied. "I have already set up an appointment with the surgeon for when we arrive in TC."

"Well what if it is APC?" she continued to push.

I told her what I knew. "It is relatively rare, with only about ten percent of patients with APC in the blood. That would mean that the cancer is loose in the blood but not yet attacking bone."

"Hopefully when we see the surgeon tomorrow we will get more complete info."

"I sure hope so."

The next day we sat before the surgeon who reviewed the reports from Dallas. "Well, 0.2 is a very low reading. We will test it again in a month. Go home and forget it until next month. Just remember that you are not authorized to worry until it reaches 0.4."

We did not forget about the problem. We were hungry for any information we could garner. We studied the books we had acquired, searched for information on the web and used contacts to locate any APC patients we might find. One month later we sat before the surgeon to review the results of a blood test.

"It is 0.4." Silence filled the room.

"Does that mean we are authorized to worry?"

"Yes. We will do another blood test in a month in order to make sure. But in the meantime we need to start thinking about alternatives for treatment."

Over the next few months, the PSA reading continued to double monthly. By early 2010, it was clear that I was at war with APC. Around this time we were shocked to learn that my surgeon would be winding down his practice to join a large Detroit group. I spent a couple of weeks interviewing doctors to manage my treatment but I was overwhelmed with the process of trying to determine a path for my treatment and felt unqualified for the task.

My previous efforts at networking to find others with APC finally paid off. Upon the recommendation of Arnie Van Zanten, the friend of a friend who also had APC, we flew to New York for a second opinion with Dr. Susan Slovin at Memorial Sloan Kettering. Since that 2010 visit she has managed my cancer treatment regimen, which involves monthly blood tests, long distance phone conversations, periodic bone scans and three or four trips per year to see her in the clinic.

Slovin's approach relies upon the least disruptive but most effective of the treatments of APC, with the goal of delaying cancer's take over. It's anticipated that, over time, a progression of more "belligerent" drugs will be needed to slow the progression of the disease. This approach is contrary to the one espoused by some doctors who would have immediately hit the cancer very hard in an attempt to beat it into a long-term remission. I chose the Sloan

Kettering approach because I felt that it would give me the most years of good living. Recently I have graduated to a stronger version of the class of drug that has been used so far. It was an uncelebrated graduation. Looking back at this strategy with full advantage of 20/20 hindsight, I would make the same decision again.

Why have I survived four major threats to my life or lifestyle? What have I learned from standing in these so-called "thin spots" where God's world and our world are close enough for us to hear God talking to us? How has the APC diagnosis changed me as a person and how might I continue to change? How should I respond to the gift of continuing life? It is certain that the cancer diagnosis has had a major effect on what is important to me. Without the diagnosis I could have continued living with a rather smug feeling that I still had the luxury of many years before me.

3

DEALING WITH REALITY

Dear Lord,
I ask that You guide me each day so that Thy will be done.

I am not the same person I was at the time of the original cancer diagnosis in 2008 and we are not the same couple we were four years ago. There are several reminders in the cottage to help me look for ways that I have changed since then: photo albums, pictures of the kids and their families, as well as a mind sated with memories and feelings of this place.

The most obvious way I have changed is the way I look. When I met Dr. Slovin the first time she told me to lose weight immediately and suggested the elimination of alcohol and red meat. On the plane back to Michigan I proposed to Anne that we go out and have a big dinner to mark the end of an era of wine, scotch and steak. She told me that the new regimen had already started and that if I didn't agree, we were going to have a problem. I agreed that we needed to implement the dietary changes immediately and that we would get back to Traverse City in time for the daily exercise and meditation regimen.

Over the next months I dropped 40 pounds. The clothes that hung in the back of the closet because they had become too tight returned to active duty. And there is no doubt that I am a calmer, more tolerant, more focused individual. I get more done. I now believe that the most effective part of the diet was the elimination of all alcohol. My increased effectiveness in the evenings has probably offset the increased time I spend sleeping due to the medication. Overall, I spend a lot less time sitting around "having one" with friends—so much so that in my mind's eye, I see an ocean going tanker with a load of scotch circling off New York Harbor as the US scotch market slumps. I feel 10 years younger than many of my peers.

In order to lessen the negative effects of stress, we simplified our lives by selling our Dallas residence after 27 years of being Texans. We moved into a large condo in Traverse City, Michigan and now enjoy the area on a year round basis. Our permanent residence is only 25 minutes from the Lake Skegemog retreat, which attracts our kids, grandchildren, and friends. The money saved by this consolidation allows for a larger participation in support of Traverse City religious, charitable and cultural activities.

By spending most of our winters in northern Michigan, we are seen as having "skin in the game" and thus have become a more significant part of the town's institutions. We feel welcome in the community and the friends we maintain are those with whom we enjoy richer conversations. Imagine talking about the legacies we want to leave versus rehashing the last Dallas Cowboys football game. The social atmosphere in Traverse City provides us with more acquaintances than we ever had in Dallas and we now have more, deeper, good friends, including the important friendships we maintain from around the country.

As a couple we are much more involved in the activities of the local Traverse City church; Anne through the parish-run indigent center and I through the church's Finance and Stewardship committees. We have become sponsors of the National Writers Series, a Traverse City based organization that gives aspiring high school writers assistance with creative writing instruction and through college scholarships. In deference to our own reading and literary interests, Anne and I have almost entirely stopped watching television so as to focus upon life's bigger issues and purposes.

Additionally, my difficulty identifying and choosing a cancer treatment, as well as the fact that I've had to travel to receive it, has led us to become significant contributors to the Munson Cancer

Center that is now being built and staffed within the local hospital. I am on the Board of the Hospital Foundation that seeks to raise about a third of the cost of this center. That this center will be of great value in our community was underlined for me this noon when the person I was eating lunch with almost came to tears as he related his experience seeking the correct treatment for his recently diagnosed cancer.

But these are not the only changes. I am in the midst of a transformation from a worshiping, rite based Christian, to a more action based Christian. This is a change in my view of the role of the organized church and of the Sunday church service, which I now realize is preparation for going out into the world and acting like a Christian by "loving thy neighbor." While it sounds like a relatively simple paradigm shift, it is an epic change for me—a redirection similar to turning a large naval vessel. It takes miles. The significance of the time it takes to make this turn is important because cancer is trying to shorten my life and I feel an urgency to identify and act upon tasks the Lord expects me to complete.

4.

DIVINE INTERVENTIONS

Dear Lord,
I thank You for the times that Your life-saving
interventions have preserved me. May I become more
mindful of your actions in my life and grow in my
understanding of the meaning of these events.

I recall four definite times that the Lord extended my useful life. The first was in September of 1945 when I had just turned four years old. Even today, 68 years later, I still feel my anxiety as the older kids walked me the mile home from school on my third day of kindergarten. They talked among themselves, largely leaving me alone as we walked along Fullerton, a busy street paralleling Grand River Avenue, one of Detroit's busiest arteries. The sounds of the kids talking mixed with the afternoon traffic noise. Eventually I saw the familiar brick pillar at the intersection of Pinehurst and Fullerton and knew it was the spot where we crossed. After that, it was an easy run past several houses to our home. My mind told me I could make it on my own. I no longer needed the older kids.

The older kids screamed as I left the curb and dashed into Fullerton traffic. I turned my head to the right just as a light green car barreled down on me. All went black as the blur of metal knocked me into the utility pole and I fell to the ground amid sounds of screeching brakes and screaming children. My next memories are of lying on a couch in our comfortable sunroom many days later. The room, jutting out from the living room toward the driveway, had windows on three sides. In the fall sunshine, the space was warm, bright and cheery. As I convalesced, I read and reread cards and drawings from Mrs. White and my kindergarten classmates. I also learned the story of what had happened after the accident.

Traffic stopped on Fullerton as police and an ambulance attended and took me to Redford Receiving Hospital, the nearest public hospital that handled emergency cases in northwestern Detroit. My situation was deemed critical and the driver of the car insisted that I receive last rites by a Catholic priest. At about the same time, Dad was arriving home from his work at Detroit Edison Company in nearby Birmingham. One of the kids who had seen the accident casually told him that an ambulance had taken me away and that my mother had gone to the hospital in a police car. After a panic call to the police and a hurried trip out Grand River, Dad arrived just in time to hear the priest finish the Eucharistic rite. I learned the story of the last rites and the angst that it had created for my parents. I was also told of differences between the Catholics and the Protestants over issues of belief and doctrines. It was all very confusing to me.

As I've thought about the accident over the years, I've come to believe that the argument of the role of the last rites in my survival is largely irrelevant. The point was that the man who hit me thought I was near death. That view was probably shared by some of the hospital staff and likely my mother. But I survived, which I feel was definitely the first instance of divine intervention. Even now, I wince at the memory of the green car in those seconds before it hit me. God had spared me.

Several years ago, after attending my uncle's funeral in Detroit, Anne and I, my brother Tom and some cousins had an opportunity to drive through that old neighborhood. Our family's small green and white house looked the same as it had in the 1940s, though the big maple tree in the backyard was gone, and a once-small tree now dominated the front yard. There were several much-used chairs on the porch to the right of the front door in the same spot where my parents would sit and talk, often waving and calling to neighbors.

But the biggest memory of that day of driving around the old neighborhood came rushing back as our car stopped at the corner of Fullerton and Pinehurst. An eight-foot tall brick monument still stood guard at the corner, a couple of steps from the utility pole and from where I ran into traffic. Staring at the monument, I had an inkling that I was looking at a marker to divine intervention in my life.

The second instance occurred when I was 10 and Tom 6, and our whole family had a near brush with death. Dad, Mother, Tom and I were fishing from a small rowboat in Skegemog, though it was called Round Lake back then. At the time, Mother was very pregnant. As we fished, a sudden surge in wind and waves came upon us and we struggled to stay afloat a hundred yards from shore. The waves finally overwhelmed the small motor and the boat tipped, dropping the anchor into about 10-12 feet of water, and effectively pinning the boat in an upside down position. We quickly paired up, joining hands, Mother with Dad and I with Tom, draping our bodies across the hull of the capsized boat. We stayed clinging to the boat as waves very slowly moved us closer to more shallow water where Dad would be able to touch bottom. Our teeth chattering in the cold wind, Dad finally touched shore as we saw a truck moving amongst nearby cherry trees. Dad told me to swim the rest of the way and get help, which I did.

We received blankets and a ride from the men in the truck. Neither Tom nor I understood the greater concern, which was for our future brother and Mother's health. A short time later, Danny was born with severe lung problems and died a couple of days later. The site of this family disaster is very near where our cottage stands today. I do not know how to relate the meaning of the sudden storm on the lake or the coincidence of the location of the boat swamping but I do know that while four of us survived, it is likely that one of us lost his life as the result of that storm.

The third time that I was spared happened almost fifteen years later in Chicago where I had moved to work for Bell & Howell Company after finishing my MBA. Together, with one of my Harvard classmates and a couple of his friends, I lived in a rented house about 20 miles from Chicago's near north side. I would often work long hours at Bell & Howell, drive downtown, drink a lot of beer and then drive back to Evanston to grab a few hours sleep before starting over early in the morning. It was probably around midnight one weekday night when I left Butch's, the largest and most renown of the Division Street bars. I found my car and headed across North Avenue to the Kennedy Expressway to drive alone on a moonless night through a darkened warehouse district where I should not have been so late at night. I do not remember seeing a red light and was shocked when a car with no highlights sped into the intersection. The other driver and I saw each other at the same point and both slammed on our breaks and spun out, narrowly avoiding the other. After the brief but loud screeching, it was absolutely quiet. My car, and I expect the other car, had stalled out. Separated by fifty yards we stared at each other before slowly leaving the scene. He did not want to talk to me any more than I wanted to talk to him. As I continued across North Avenue, shaking and sweaty, I realized that two lives had been spared, mine for a third time. I drove slowly and extra carefully as I relived the near tragedy several times in my mind. Surely, I would have to change my ways.

Shortly thereafter, I was diagnosed with Mononucleosis, the "kissing disease," a likely result of burning the candle at both ends. I returned to my parent's home in Birmingham for six weeks of convalescence and reflection. Why had I been spared? Although I had no answer to the question, I had a changed outlook. I moved out of the house in Evanston and into a room on the near north side of Chicago.

In 2002, I had yet a fourth brush with what could have resulted in death. I had flown from Dallas to Houston to attend a major oil business reception at the magnificent Museum of Natural History. Amidst large exhibits of prehistoric animals in authentic settings there was the clink of wine glasses and the smell of extravagant food. Many of the exhibits were sponsored by businesses represented by the 400 guests who comprised the leadership of the exploration and production segment of the oil industry. I enjoyed the first few minutes of mingling and talking but began to feel seriously nauseated. I said the obligatory thank you and left.

The next morning I returned to Dallas, still a little shaken but I seemed well enough to go straight to work. At about eleven, I called the Chief Financial Officer of the Dallas based company that had given the party the prior night and we agreed to meet for lunch at a deli we both frequented. As we ate cheeseburgers, he told me that he had just been diagnosed with MS and would be beginning a chemical treatment regimen that would attempt to keep the disease from intensifying. As I listened to him, I felt the room grow warm and my vision become unstable. He stopped talking and said I looked terrible. He picked up my keys, left money on the table and helped me to my feet. Ten minutes later I was in the emergency room of a large hospital.

Throughout the afternoon one test followed another. Around 6:30 pm, a doctor entered the room and pointed his finger between my eyes and said, "You are one sick puppy. I don't have any idea why you almost fainted but it probably saved your life. You are on your way to the cardiac unit where your heart will be monitored until Monday, when we can take a look inside to determine how to address what is likely a significant artery blockage."

As usual in this type of emergency, Anne was calm and reassuring. She picked up my clothes, thanked the Doctor and began asking questions to further our knowledge of the situation while I sat dejectedly on the examination table. As we were to go to an important social engagement that weekend, I argued to allow me to take it easy at home over the weekend and return to the hospital on Monday. My feeble attempt to change the plan was immediately dismissed by both Anne and the doctor. A catheterization was performed on Monday morning and I awoke to find Anne talking to two doctors about a double bypass operation that would soon follow, since the in-heart investigation had shown a 90% plus blockage in the left main descending artery—the so-called "widow maker." The operation was successful and as I rested at home, I thought about the meaning of this latest brush with death, feeling that the hand of God had once again intervened to save my life.

After the APC diagnosis in 2009 I went through a very dark period while I searched for an oncologist to direct my treatment. Eventually I met Arnie Van Zanten through one of my fraternity brothers, and he connected me to the competent care that I am fortunate to be receiving at Sloan Kettering. I feel that the events involved with meeting Arnie and finding Dr. Susan Slovin have been just as important in prolonging my life as the other four life saving events prior to my cancer diagnosis.

5

INFLECTION POINTS AND THIN SPOTS

Dear Lord,
Please help me to understand the meaning of Your
interventions in my life that I may heed your instructions.

An inflection point is a concept in math that describes the exact location of a change in direction, usually seen as a flat spot of a curve drawn on graph paper. Think of the arc of a rocket as it rapidly ascends, gradually slows, flattens and turns back toward the earth. The exact point at which the rocket stops climbing, flattens out and begins to fall is the inflection point. Throughout history, lives have been altered by wars, famines, economic cycles, political events, deaths, births and many other chance occurrences. I believe that the four near-miss events in my life have formed important inflection or pivot points, functioning in a similar way to change my course. These particular points appear in contrast to the slow acting, long term changes that one's life incurs. These extended process changes include both mental and physical maturation, education, transfer of family values from parent to child, the long-term effect of a religious upbringing, and the growth of a marriage relationship, to name a few.

Divine communications might be referred to as happening within the context of the historical concept of "thin-spots." The idea is that occasionally the separation between the divine and physical world becomes very narrow or thin. At these rare and fleeting times, we receive communications from the divine. The ancient Scottish concept has these events occurring in specific locations, for example, a certain grove of trees. I believe that the physical place of the occurrence is not important and instead, a thin spot can be anywhere. What is important is that the mental state of the intended communicant must be open to receiving messages and leadership. There are likely many times in my life where, had I been in the proper frame of mind, I would likely have received additional directional nudges. I am hopeful that daily meditation and prayer will keep me receptive to receiving any messages that are meant for me.

What follows are my notes upon returning from a mission trip to Central America and describe my most powerful experience at a thin spot.

JANUARY, 2007, LA CEIBA, HONDURAS

The small boy's dark eyes looked up at me as if he were seeing through my body. Amidst the din of the crowd in the courtyard, he pointed to the small wooden cross and nametag that hung around my neck. In spite of the noise, I heard him speak clearly in English, "Are you a Christian?"

We locked eyes and I responded, "Yes." He nodded and in an instant was gone into the crowd while I stood transfixed in the courtyard of the overcrowded clinic. No one had ever asked me that question before! I thought of how much easier it was for me to answer affirmatively than it had been for the Apostle Peter when his life had been on the line in a similar courtyard 2000 years ago.

The heart of our mission to Honduras is the clinic. Our group included four doctors and three nurses, supported by a number of "non-pro" workers in triage and pharmacy. Two Honduran doctors joined the team, and several additional Hondurans helped control the crowds that were desperately seeking care.

The clinic is physically remote from the church and the school by being located in the barrio where most kids would not usually have access to regular medical attention and often come from poor families who can't afford to send their children to school, either. It opens only one week a year, when our mission team opens it. The work in the clinic is done in conjunction with the local Holy Trinity Episcopal Church and School where the construction and teaching crews worked.

When my construction colleagues and I took a break and went to the clinic in order to see the care being provided to the district's residents by our fellow team members, we saw a line of about 100 kids and parents within the courtyard. The line to enter the courtyard was at least that long. As I looked at the calmness of people awaiting treatment, my mind returned the short lines at doctors' offices I've used. I felt heavy with gratitude for my circumstance and for the chance to be of service to these people.

As we returned to our work site by riding in the rear of an old pick-up truck, I continued to see and hear the boy. He was a slightly brown boy, about 5 feet tall, wearing sandals, blue shorts, and a white t-shirt. He spoke to me in clear English. As the truck bounced along the road full of potholes, I pondered what had been so special about the week, and was thankful that the child with the piercing eyes had chosen to speak to me, striking a responsive chord that I will long remember for its clarity.

After thinking about the week and the boy for some time, I've concluded that the hard physical work I did in La Ceiba had truly been service in God's kingdom. I had given of myself in a way that was unique for me. The tiring labor had me working by rote, which is what often happens when I do repetitive work. My mind wanders and by not focusing, becomes receptive to new thoughts, ideas or communications. Our encounter was over so very quickly, but it was unmistakable.

As I got off the plane in Dallas I was still thinking about the incident and realized that I was one of the last of our group still wearing my small wooden cross and nametag. It was an emotional moment when I removed it and put it in my bag, an indication that it was time to return to my world of plenty, and life of meetings and business travel. I would miss the necklace serving as a reminder of my encounter with the divine, speaking with God through the boy.

It is my hope that the cross and nametag, now hanging in my den, remain constant reminders of three things: I am a Christian and must try to contribute to God's kingdom here on earth; I should tell as many people as possible about the great rewards garnered with service to those needing help; and I should be alert for the next time I come face to face with a thin spot where the question is "Are you a Christian?" I took the message to be a very pointed direction to me that my life should be a much clearer sign of what it means to be a Christian; a life of service and loving my neighbor.

I recently had another thin spot communication. In this experience, I saw the small boy staring at me during a stewardship meeting at our church. He didn't speak. He did not need to speak. At the time he reappeared, we were talking about the need for the members of the committee to give individual testimonials before the congregation. These statements were planned to be very personal. As the conversation progressed, I began to think of a statement that might sidestep the central idea of committing to higher levels of giving. The reappearance of the boy was a strong message to me to give a statement that was firm and showed commitment. A month later, as I spoke before my fellow congregants, I thought of the boy and was thankful that I had again received his message.

6

RESPONDING TO THE MESSAGE

Dear Lord,
Help me to feel Your presence, hear Your message,
and do Your will.

Most people are familiar with the Old Testament story of Abram, the founding character of Jewish and Christian and Muslim religious faiths. In this story, the Lord intervenes several times in Abram's life, including when his name changes to Abraham and he becomes the leader of a great nation. But, probably the best known of the Lord's New Testament interventions is when the Lord talks with Saul on his way to Damascus. Saul not only changes his name to Paul but he becomes the leading messenger of Christianity to the Gentile world.

In both of these stories, the Lord directly charges a person to change his life and to accomplish specific tasks. While difficult, the assigned task included an understandable objective. However, I am most drawn to the story of an unnamed blind man in Bethsaida whose sight was restored by Jesus in Mark 8:22 – 26. In this story, the blind man is brought to Jesus who restores his vision and tells him to go directly home. While Jesus has provided a huge inflection point for this man, the man receives no instructions on what he should do with his gift of a better life with sight. Jesus has left it up to the man to interpret the meaning of this glorious gift.

I can imagine the formerly blind man talking with a wife, son and daughter-in-law about the meaning of the gift. He probably talked to the beggars whom he sat with during the years of begging under the blistering sun at the dusty city gates. I think that many discussions would have revolved around the concept of a debt owed for the gift. Alternately, some would have thought that he should focus upon working for those less fortunate than himself, out of thanks and joy over the healing.

Had I the chance to talk with the man, I would have taken the latter position. I do not think Jesus wanted the man to feel a debt or any guilt. Instead, Jesus would have wanted the man to serve his community, which I would define as the blind beggars at the city gate. He could have done this by working for pay during the day, and using his income and free time to serve the others as a testament to his life.

As I ponder the ways that I can use my time, I do not feel a sense of guilt or debt associated with my life. I'm appreciative for the divine interventions and for the resulting period of extended, or new life that I have before me. The Lord is helping me fight the cancer by providing me the necessary family, financial and medical resources, positive outlook and faith in a continuation of a fruitful life. I also believe that I am meant to do something more and that is why I have repeatedly been given life extensions. I am keenly sensitive to finding and completing my mission, as I believe it is the Lord's plan for me.

7.

My New Life

Dear Lord,
Help me understand the concept of "New Life"
and to use my time in the manner that You intend.

It is 4:26 a.m. I went to bed last night after spending the afternoon and evening trying to summarize my feelings about my new life and how I will use the time afforded to me. Through the night, I tossed and turned until the solution arrived. I quietly arose, made coffee and have now begun to put what I sought into words.

My new life began when the reality of the cancer diagnosis sank in. Life will never be the same as I will always live with the threat of an early death. I may have times of remission but never again will I be "cancer free." I plan to use a few minutes each day for meditation. If the Lord wants to talk to me, I want to make sure that I am listening.

There is a sense of satisfaction with the changes that have occurred since this new life began. I will resist urges to backslide and return to drinking alcohol. The pounds that have been shed will stay off. Anne and I will continue to simplify our living as we have already begun to do by selling the Dallas house. These changes are concrete and are easy to see, touch and feel. But even in their entirety, they are like the overture before an opera.

I will continue to strengthen my relationships with my family, primarily with Anne, our children and grandchildren. These feelings are probably among the first felt by anyone given a cancer diagnosis. They form a path to being remembered after you are gone. This Spring my 12 year-old grandson Alex, and I, went on a ten-day trip to the Galapagos Islands. We had a wonderful bonding experience. I will never forget Alex's focus on photography, a focus rewarded by his receiving the ship's prize for taking the best photo. Several days from now Alex, his sister, his mother, and Anne and I will be in Chicago for a weekend of theater and exploration. The trip will be a wonderful opportunity for us to strengthen family ties that can loosen with our geographical separation. Closeness is important as we approach the holiday season

Anne and I have had a strong relationship with the Episcopal Church since our marriage 46 years ago, and have been involved in a lot of wonderful ministries, though I am feeling frustrated by involvement through committee as opposed to dealing directly with those needing assistance. I need to stay awake, alert and available to persons and situations that I may help with my time or treasure. I have identified two areas where I might serve people on a personal basis. One of these possibilities is as a Stephen's Minister. These Ministers meet weekly with those in the community that are lonely and in the need of visitation to "talk things through." My dad had weekly visits from Stephen's Ministers for years and those visits were the highlights of his week. I would like to be a catalyst in starting such a program within our church and follow through by being one such minister myself. I might cast some brotherhood into someone's life.

A second opportunity, serving those with a cancer diagnosis, came before me during my last visit to the Sloan-Kettering. I was in the reception area, waiting to be called and I could not help but become aware of the extremely anxious couple sitting across from me. They conversed about the man's APC diagnosis and about the difficulty they experienced getting to the clinic from nearby Queens. The man responded to the call to have his blood sample drawn and as soon as he walked into the lab, his wife came over and sat next to me. We talked in hushed tones. This was their first visit to the clinic. Her husband had just been diagnosed with APC but still had a very low PSA reading. I didn't say much to her but assured her that they were in the right place. I suggested a couple of books that would give her some of the background that they needed. It was not until my name was called, and I stood, that I realized she had a tight grip on my arm and was hanging on my every word. That encounter left me with a sense of the value of community among patients, and how important it is for me to help others whenever the chance presents itself.

Three weeks ago, I lost my closest link to that community when my friend Arnie Van Zanten died. I was devastated. Today, as I slowly pack my pencils, pads and computer and prepare to depart the cottage, the last thing I do is write a eulogy for Arnie.

AMEM

ACKNOWLEDGEMENTS

Of the many people who helped to create this story, I particularly thank my family and friends.

Bob and Jean Montgomery were wonderful parents who gave all they could to my brother Tom and me. Tom has always stood at my side, including when I organized these thoughts.

It has been one of life's great experiences to walk with our children Alyson, John and Chris as they matured and found their places in the world. We love telling the family story to our grandchildren.

Many friends have been long-term shapers of my life experience and this manuscript. There are too many to name but they know who they are and all they have meant.

My sincere appreciation goes to Holly Wren Spaulding for her help in getting this story into print.

Finally I give thanks that the Lord gave me Anne as a life partner and best friend. My life would not have been the same without her.

Biography

Bill Montgomery graduated from the University of Michigan with an honors degree in Economics and earned his Masters of Business Administration degree from Harvard University. He enjoyed a long career, working in several facets of the oil and gas industry. He and his wife Anne live in Traverse City, Michigan where they are avid volunteers, readers and often travel to Texas and New Hampshire to visit their children and grandchildren.

Bill Montgomery can be reached at bmonty5@gmail.com.

Made in the USA
Charleston, SC
13 August 2014